ARTS & CRAFTS SAMPLER
from Evan-Moor

P9-ECZ-471

Enjoy using these activities from Evan-Moor arts and crafts titles. We hope that they will enrich your instructional program, show you how effective and easy-to-use our materials are, and encourage you to try some of the many arts and crafts titles for Grades K–6 published by Evan-Moor.

▼ ▼ ▼ ▼ The Activities ▼ ▼ ▼ ▼

Note: Each activity displays the grade level designation of the book from which it is taken. Many activities, however, may be appropriate for a wider grade span.

▲ ▲ ▲ ▲ ▲ ▲ ▲ ▲ ▲ ▲ ▲ ▲ ▲

Evan-Moor
EDUCATIONAL PUBLISHERS

EMC 057

Arts and Crafts

Quick and Easy Crafts Your Students Will Love

Complete, Illustrated Step-by-Step Directions

Crafts for Young Children
Grades PreK–1
40 age-appropriate arts and crafts projects using paint, paper, crayon, and other media. Materials list, step-by-step illustrated directions, and reproducible patterns provided.
80 pp.   **$7.95**   **EMC 720**

Folk Art Projects – North America
Grades 1–6
18 projects based on folk art styles from the Far North, Americana, Native American groups, and Mexico/Central America.
80 pp.   **$7.95**   **EMC 724**

Folk Art Projects – Around the World
Grades 1–6
29 projects from Africa, the Americas, Asia, and Europe. Cultural background and literature references with each project.
80 pp.   **$7.95**   **EMC 721**

Paper Crafts
Grades 1–6
31 projects to create decorations, hats, masks, and 3-D designs.
80 pp.   **$7.95**   **EMC 723**

How to Make Greeting Cards with Children
Grades 1–6
Create 38 delightful holiday and special-occasion cards. Styles of cards include pop-up, accordion fold, and more.
80 pp.   **$7.95**   **EMC 231**

Paper Tube Zoo
Grades K–3
Revised & Expanded! Recycle those leftover toilet paper tubes into 36 delightful animals. Reproducible patterns make the projects easy to assemble.
80 pp.   **$7.95**   **EMC 771**

Folded Paper Projects
Grades 1–6
Revised and Expanded! Make 39 charming projects from just 11 basic folds. Use them as puppets, to motivate writing, as decorations, and more.
80 pp.   **$7.95**   **EMC 772**

Holiday Art Projects
Grades 1–6
37 festive projects. Information on the holidays is included. Cut paper, 3-D constructions, printing, weaving, and more.
80 pp.   **$7.95**   **EMC 722**

How to Make Puppets with Children
Grades 1–6
Easy-to-follow directions and all necessary patterns for making 37 hand puppets and 26 alphabet finger puppets.
80 pp.   **$7.95**   **EMC 762**

Sandcasting

This activity is the most fun if done at the beach, of course! However, a sandbox or a plastic tub full of sand works just as well. This can be messy, so smocks and a well-covered floor are a good idea.

Materials

- sand
- large plastic tub
- plaster of Paris
- small shells, pebbles, driftwood
- spoons
- bucket or can for mixing plaster of Paris
- water
- clean, stiff paintbrush
- large paper clips (optional)
- water

Steps to Follow

1. Moisten the sand (until damp, not wet). Using hands and spoons, form a design in the sand. Don't make it too deep or too large, otherwise it will take forever to dry. A couple of inches (5 cm) deep and six inches (15 cm) or so wide is a nice size. Simple shapes such as a sea star, scallop shell, sun, or fish work best.

2. Add details by drawing in the sand. You may also place shells, pebbles and/or bits of driftwood in the hole to form part of your design.

3. Mix plaster of Paris according to the directions on the package. Pour the liquid plaster into the hole, filling it just to the surface. Let the sandcasting dry undisturbed. The drying time will depend on how large a sandcasting has been made.

   If you wish to hang the sandcastings, add a large paper clip "hook" when the sandcasting has set somewhat, but before it has dried completely.

4. Carefully lift the dry sandcasting from the sand. Brush off the excess sand and admire your wonderful creation!

A Pie Pan Mobile

Take a walk and collect nature's treasures to hang on your mobile.

materials

- aluminum foil pan (tart or potpie size)

- raffia

- 1" (2.5 cm) square of cardboard

- treasures to hang

- paper name tag

- hole punch

Steps to follow ➤

1. Punch two holes in the cardboard square.

2. Center the cardboard square inside the pan. Mark the spots where the holes are. Have an adult poke two holes in the pie pan where the marks are.

3. Thread a 12" (30 cm) piece of raffia down through the one hole in the pan and the cardboard square and back up through the other hole.

   Tie the raffia together close to the pan and then again at the end to create a hanging loop. (Using the cardboard square will prevent the aluminum foil from tearing when you hang your mobile.)

4. Punch holes at even distances around the edge of the pan.

5. Put raffia through each hole.

6. Tie treasures to the raffia pieces.

7. Punch a hole in the name tag, and thread a piece of raffia through the hole. Pass the raffia under the loop on the inside center of the pan and knot.

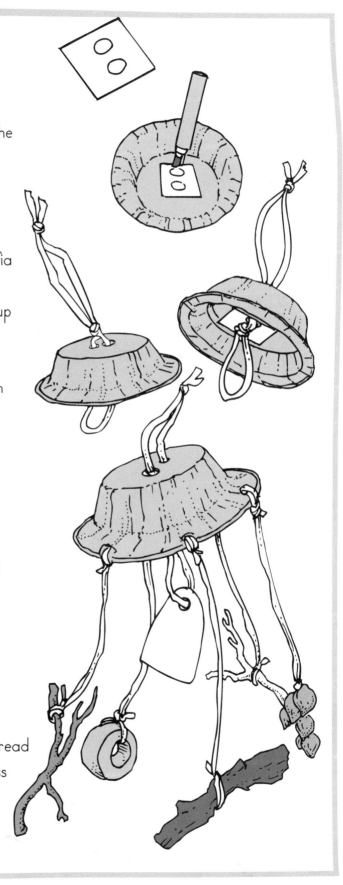

Cornstarch Clay Penguin

Cornstarch clay is a pure white clay. It will air-dry in several days and can be baked in the oven at low temperatures if you want it to harden more quickly.

materials

- saucepan
- stove top or hot plate
- spoon
- cutting board
- cookie sheet
- black, white, and yellow tempera paint
- paintbrushes
- cotton swabs

Ingredients for 10 to 15 penguins

- 1 cup cornstarch
- 2 cups baking soda
- 1 1/3 cups water

Steps to follow ➤

Making the Clay

1. Put the water into a pan. Stir over medium heat as you add the cornstarch and baking soda. When the mixture is like mashed potatoes remove it from heat.

2. Pour onto a cutting board to cool. As soon as the dough is cool enough, knead it.

3. Keep the clay in an airtight container when you are not working with it. It will keep for several weeks.

Forming the Penguin

1. Roll a 2" (5cm) diameter ball of clay in your hand.

2. Shape it into a fat log.

3. Pinch a beak out of the front of the log.

4. Pinch a wing out of each side.

5. Let the penguin dry or bake it until it's hard in a 300° oven.

Painting the Penguin

1. Paint the penguin black. Let dry.

2. Dip a thumb in thick white paint to "paint" penguin's tummy.

3. Dip the tip of a cotton swab in white paint to make eyes. When dry add the pupil with black marker.

4. Paint the penguin's beak yellow.

Paper Tube Zoo

Frog

1. Cover the tube with green paper.
2. Color the frog patterns.
3. Cut out the patterns and glue them on the tube.

Glue the legs to the side of the tube.

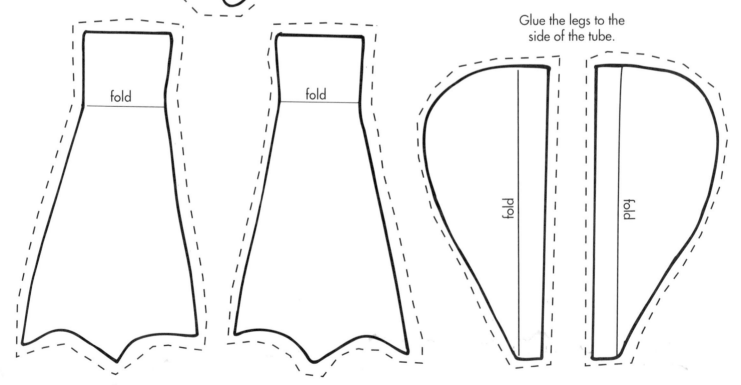

fold

fold

fold

fold

Place your
Paper Tube Zoo
friend here.

Frog

Its webbed feet swim.
Its strong legs hop.
Carrying frog
From spot to spot.

Write about your animal.

_____

_____

_____

_____

_____

_____

_____

_____

Paper Tube Zoo

Name:

Stuffed Paper Creations

Stuffing is a quick way to create large, colorful works of art. Begin with this "fishy" lesson, then move on to create rainforests, gardens, parades, etc., of "stuffed" creations.

▶ **Materials**

- butcher paper - 18" x 24" (45.5 x 61 cm) - 2 sheets per child
- construction paper scraps - many colors
- marking pens or crayons
- scissors
- glue
- stapler

Optional - Found objects such as buttons, rickrack, ribbon, bottle caps, etc., to use for eyes and scales. Glitter to add sparkle to the fish.

Steps to Follow

1. Sketch the outline of a fish on one sheet of butcher paper. Keep it simple. Fancy fins can be added from scraps later on.

2. Cut out two fish exactly the same shape and size.

3. Decorate both fish exactly the same.

4. Tear newspaper into strips to use as stuffing.

5. Staple or glue the tail fin sections together along the edge. Stuff the fins with newspaper. (If you use glue, let the fish dry before you try to stuff it.)

6. Staple or glue the sides of the fish and stuff the body with newspaper.

7. Staple or glue around the mouth area to close off the fish.

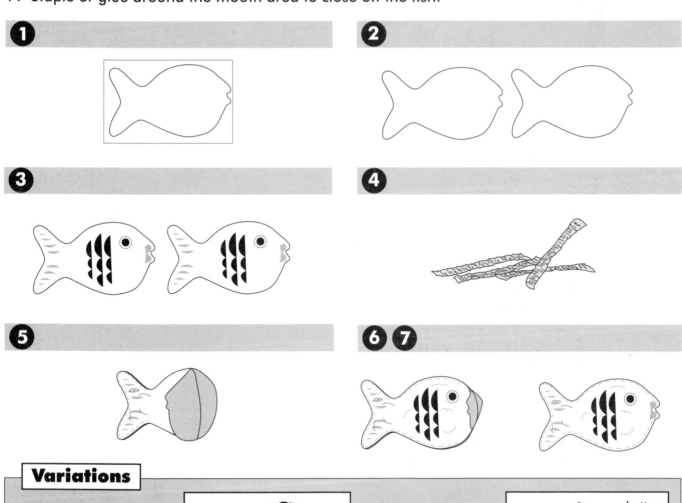

1

2

3

4

5

6 7

Variations

Punch holes around the outside edge of the fish. Lace it together using yarn.

Cut a fish from felt. Sew it together with a large plastic needle and yarn.

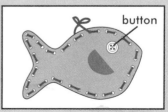

button

Crocodile

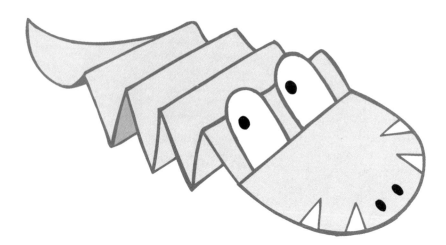

Materials

- green paper rectangle–3" x 10" (7.5 x 25.5 cm)
- 2 white paper rectangles–1" x 2" (2.5 x 5 cm)
- yellow paper scraps
- black marking pen
- scissors
- glue

Ways to Use

- Use as a border for a bulletin board displaying stories or reports about reptiles, swamps, or crocodiles.

- Read *Lyle, Lyle, Crocodile* by Bernard Waber. Retell the story in writing. Glue the crocodile and story to a large sheet of blue construction paper.

- Use your crocodile as a bookmark when reading stories or nonfiction books about crocodiles or other reptiles.

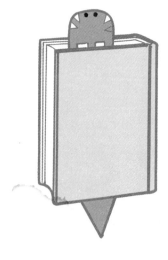

Steps to Follow

1 Round the corners on one end of the rectangle. Cut the other end to a point.

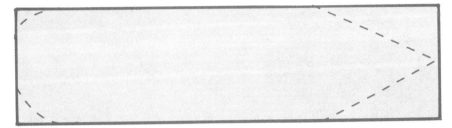

2 Fold back the snout section.

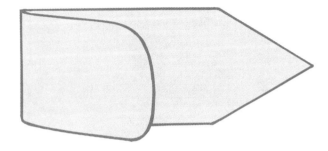

3 Accordion-fold the middle of the crocodile's body.

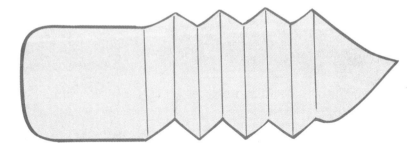

4 Round two corners of the white rectangles. Glue these eyes to the first fold. Add eyeballs and nostrils with the marking pen. Cut little yellow teeth from scrap paper and glue them around the snout.

Paper Bag Portraits

Create a mosaic portrait using torn colored-paper bags.

Vocabulary

mosaic

portrait

Materials

- lightweight cardboard (any size)
- white glue mixed with a small amount of water
- paintbrushes for glue
- colorful paper bags
- cups
- pencils

Project Notes

- For this project collect paper bags with different colors printed on them: pet food bags, grocery bags, old gift bags, etc.
- Show portraits done by famous artists and compare their styles.
- Talk about placement of facial features to help children plan their portraits.

Let's Talk About It

How is a mosaic different from a painted portrait?

What other materials could be used to create a portrait?

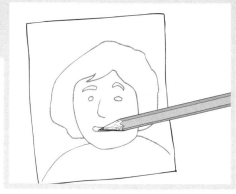

step 1

step 2

step 3

step 4

Steps to Follow

1 Draw a simple portrait of a friend. Sketch it in pencil on the cardboard. Use an oval for the face and add the eyebrows, eyes, nose, and mouth. Keep it simple.

2 Tear the bags into small pieces. Sort the pieces into piles by color. Children can plan what colors and textures they will use in their mosaic.

3 Brush glue on the background area. Then place the colored bag pieces on the glue. Continue until the background is completely covered by using the brush to help smooth pieces down. Keep fingers clean. The glue will dry clear. It is a good idea to overlap pieces.

4 Apply the glue to the hair and then add the torn paper.

5 Now begin on the face. Place the pieces of torn paper to follow the contours of the face. After the "skin" is covered, fill in the lips, eyes, and eyebrows. Tear the colored pieces to fit the small areas such as eyes and lips.

6 Add clothing, a hat, or other details.

7 Make sure all the paper pieces are glued securely. Set the mosaic aside to dry.

Hippo
Folded Paper Puppet

Materials

- 9" x 18" (23 x 45.5 cm) gray construction paper
- patterns on page 17
- marking pens or crayons
- scissors
- glue

Steps to Follow

1. Make the basic folded puppet out of the construction paper.

a.

Fold in thirds.

b.

Fold in half.

Fold top edge back. Flip over and fold back other side.

c.

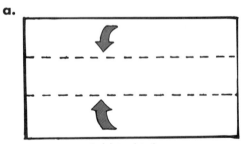

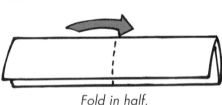

Put fingers in open spaces.

2. Color the pattern pieces and cut them out.

3. Glue the patterns to the folded paper puppet.

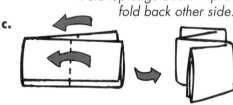

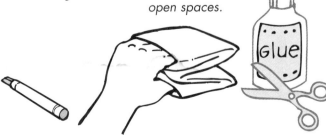

4. Add nostrils with crayons or markers.

Folded Paper Puppet Patterns

fold

gray ears with
pink centers

fold

fold

gray legs with pink toes

fold

white teeth

fold   *fold*

eyes

pink
tongue

New Year's Day

New Year's Day is a time to celebrate the end of the old year and the beginning of a new year. All over the world the new year is welcomed with great noise. In ancient times, people believed that noise would scare away evil spirits and make room for spirits bringing good luck.

While we celebrate the new year on January 1, cultures using different calendars celebrate at other times of the year.

Noisemakers

Make noisemakers from paper bowls and paper towel tubes.

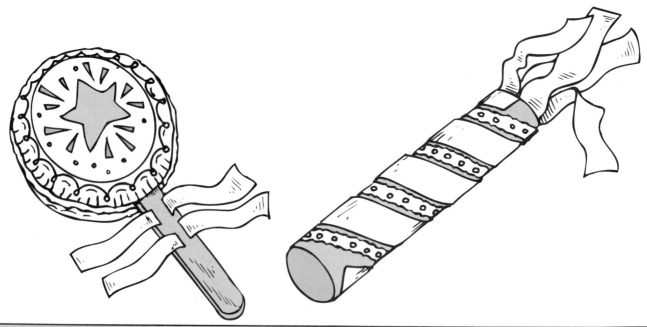

Materials

Shakers
- 2 paper soup bowls
- pebbles, beans, or nuts in their shells
- glue (tacky glue works best)
- scissors
- tongue depressor
- marking pens
- 4 tissue or crepe paper strips -
  1" x 4" (2.5 x 10 cm)

"Ta-Da" Tubes
- paper towel roll
- construction paper -
  6" x 12" (15 x 30.5 cm)
- 1 tissue or crepe paper strip -
  1 1/2" x 18" (3.8 x 45.5 cm)
- 4 tissue or crepe paper strips -
  1" x 9" (2.5 x 26 cm)
- glue, marking pens, scissors

New Year's Noisemakers

Tip:
Encourage children to assist each other when they reach a place where extra hands are helpful.

Steps to Follow

Shakers

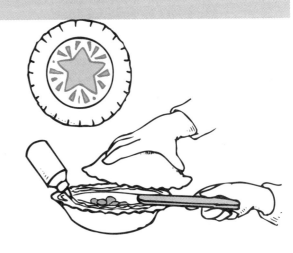

1. Decorate the bottoms of the paper bowls using marking pens.

2. Put a handful of pebbles, beans, or nuts in one of the paper bowls. Spread a layer of glue around the edge of the bowl.

3. Have a second person hold the tongue depressor in place. Put glue on top of the tongue depressor. Place the other bowl on top. Hold the tongue depressor steady as the glue dries.

4. Glue two streamers to each side of the tongue depressor. When the glue is dry, shake the rattle as you celebrate the coming of the new year.

"Ta-Da" Tubes

1. Place glue along one edge of the construction paper rectangle. Lay the tube along the same edge. Wrap the paper around the tube and glue the other edge in place.

2. Glue the end of the 18" (45.5 cm) paper strip to one end of the tube. Wind the strip around the tube and glue it to the other end.

3. Add other decorations to the tube using marking pens.

4. Glue the remaining strips to one end of the tube.

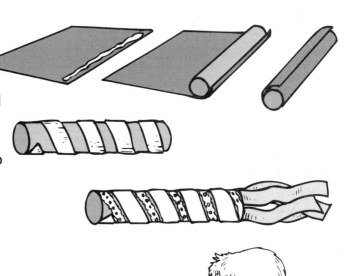

5. When the glue is dry blow through the tube and shout "Ta-Da!"

You're So Nice

Materials

- pattern (page 21) reproduced on card stock or construction paper
- Exacto® knife (adult use only)
- 8" (20 cm) piece of ribbon
- small self-closing plastic bag
- hole punch
- crayons; scissors

Steps to follow

1. Cut out the pattern. Cut the inside lines with an Exacto® knife.

2. Fold on the lines.

3. Write "Thank You" on the front. Then pull card open and it says "You're So Nice."

4. Decorate the outside frame with a border design.

5. Put the finished card into a plastic bag. Punch a hole in the corner of the plastic bag. Fold ribbon in half and push the loop through the hole. Pull the ends through the loop and tie a knot at the end.

Optional

Use stick-on dots, colorful stickers, or permanent felt markers to decorate the plastic bag.

Pattern for card

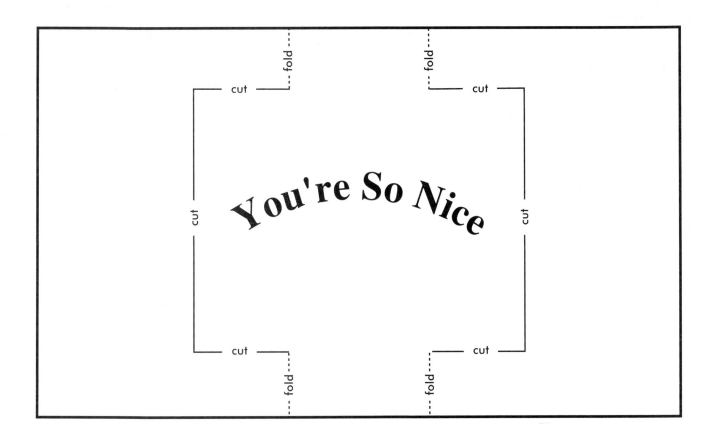

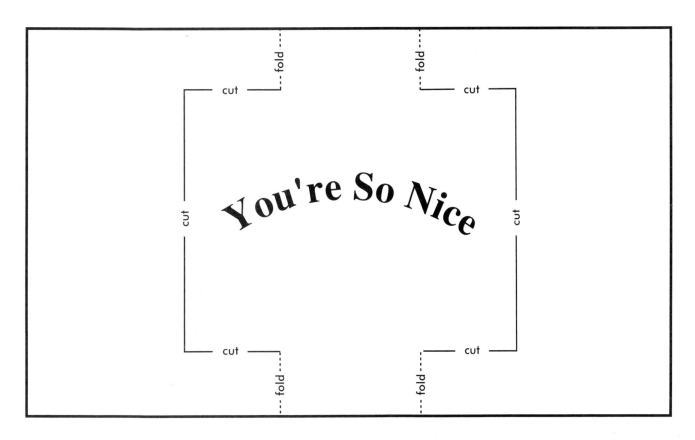

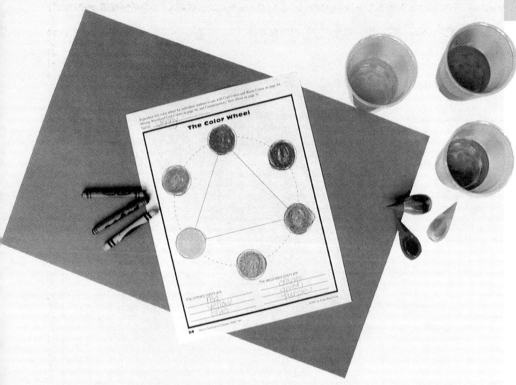

Secondary Colors

The primary colors can be mixed to create the secondary colors of orange, green, and violet.

Step by Step

1. Place the three small jars of primary colors on the overhead projector in the positions shown on the color wheel sheet. Add three empty jars in the positions of the secondary colors.

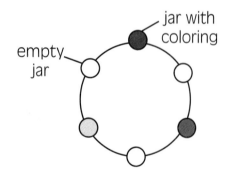

empty jar

jar with coloring

2. Use an eyedropper to mix the primary colors, creating secondary colors in the empty jars. Stir to mix. Always begin with the lightest color and add the darker color one drop at a time.

3. When all the mixing is complete, you will have created the three secondary colors—purple, orange, and green.

4. Have students use colored pencils or crayons and the color wheel sheet to show how the secondary colors are made.

Note: In this book the word purple is used instead of violet as it is the word commonly used on classroom crayons, construction paper, and paint.

Materials

• food coloring and water premixed in glass jars for the three primary colors—red, blue, and yellow

• small glass bowls or plastic glasses

• three eyedroppers

• overhead projector

• color wheel sheet on page 23, reproduced for individual students

• colored pencils or crayons

Name _____

The Color Wheel

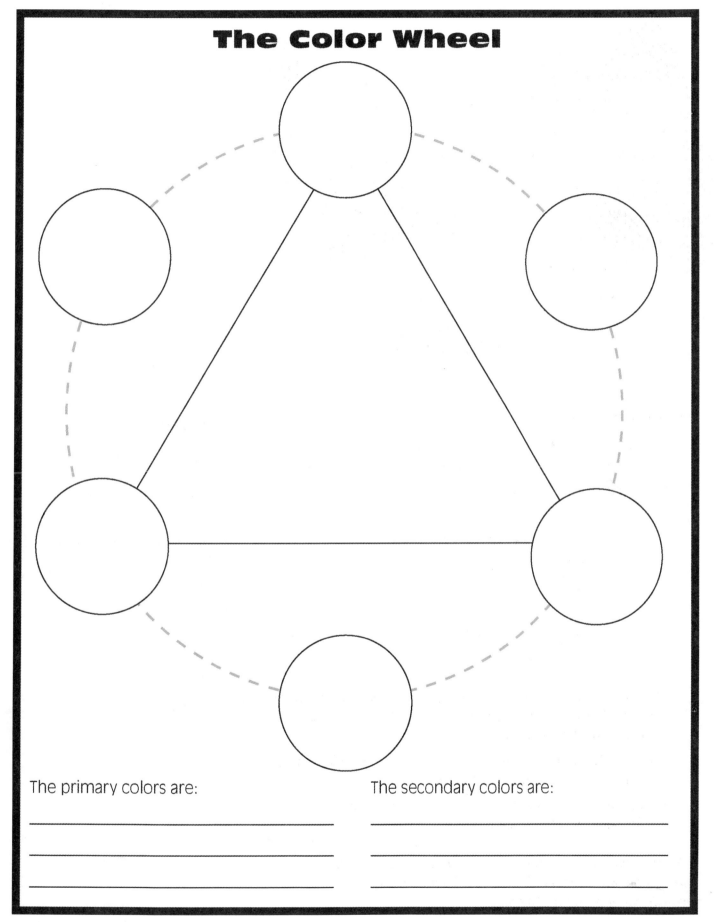

The primary colors are:

_____

_____

_____

The secondary colors are:

_____

_____

_____

Make a Slinky Snake

This "hiss-terical" snake is a great favorite of children of all ages.

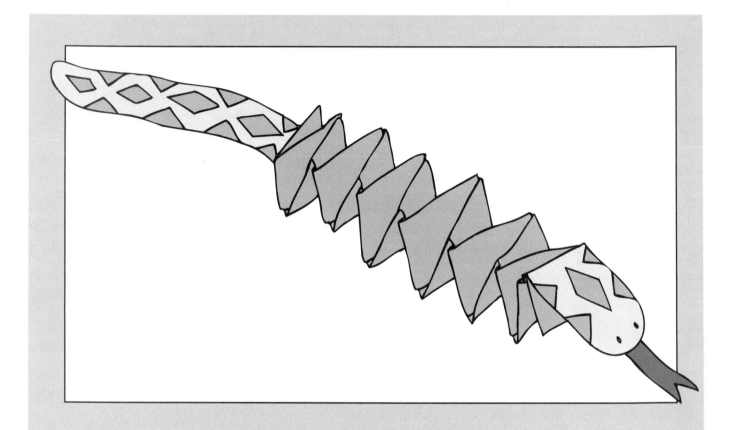

▶ Materials

- green paper strips–1" x 18" (2.5 x 45.5 cm)–2 per snake
- yellow paper strip–1" x 12" (2.5 x 30.5 cm)
- scrap of red paper at least 2" (5 cm) long
- scissors
- glue
- crayons
- ruler

▶ Jacob's Ladder

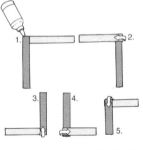

1. Lay the two strips as shown and glue together.
2. Fold the top strip across to the left.
3. Fold the bottom strip up.
4. Fold the left strip to the right.
5. Fold the top strip down.
6. Continue until you reach the end of the strips. Cut off any excess and glue the ends together.

Steps to Follow

1. Make a Jacob's Ladder (page 24) with the two green strips.

2. Cut 3" (7.5 cm) off the yellow strip. Draw the snake's head. Cut it out.

3. Draw a tail on the rest of the strip. Draw scales on the tail. Cut it out.

4. Cut a forked tongue out of the red scrap.

5. Glue the parts together.

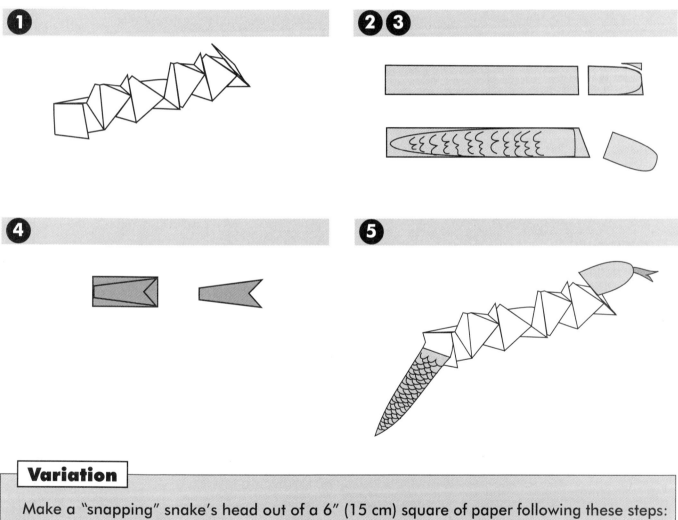

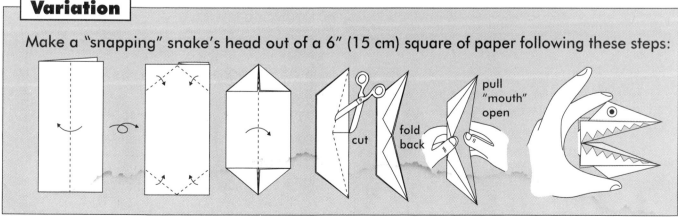

Variation

Make a "snapping" snake's head out of a 6" (15 cm) square of paper following these steps:

Make Bark Pictures—Australia

▶ Steps to Follow

1. Tear the edges of a piece of brown wrapping paper or a large brown grocery bag. This rough edged paper will be your bark.

2. Lay the torn paper over the wood and rub a dark brown or black crayon over the paper. Pick up as much of the pattern of the wood grain as possible. This is called a relief print.

3. Using crayons or markers draw a simple Australian animal on the bark print (or use templates on page 27). Divide animal into a number of design areas. Fill in each area with lines and dots.

4. Glue the finished bark drawing onto a larger piece of construction paper.

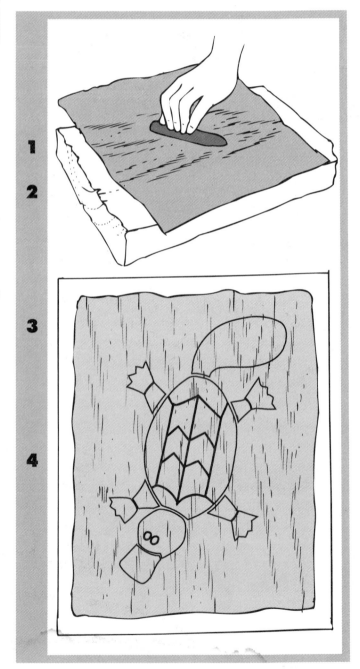

If your students need larger figures, enlarge these patterns with your copier before making templates.

Textured Paint Collage

Students cut apart textured paint papers they have created and make new simple collage pictures.

Materials

(for each student)

- white construction paper—

  4" x 6" (10 x 15 cm)

  three 4" (10 cm) squares

- acrylic paints

- flat-ended paintbrush

- scraps of cardboard

- plastic fork, plastic knife, comb (any object that will help to create a texture)

- scissors

- glue

Step by Step

1. Squeeze a small amount of paint onto each 4" square.

2. Allow students to experiment with creating different textures on each of their color squares.

3. Let the painted squares dry completely.

4. Brainstorm simple picture or design ideas that can be cut free-form from the squares.

5. Glue the shapes to the white construction paper.

Make Star Streamers—Japan

▶ **Materials**

- squares of origami paper or gift wrap
  —4 1/2" (11.5 cm)
- a stick about 2 feet (60 cm) long
- a needle with a large eye
- three 18" (45.5 cm) lengths of thin string
- beads or Cheerios

▶ **Steps to Follow**

1. To make one paper triangle:
   - Fold the paper square (colored side in) in half to make a rectangle. (Crease all folds well.)
   - Fold the rectangle in half again to make a small square.
   - Unfold completely.
   - Fold in half diagonally.
   - Unfold and fold in half diagonally the other way.
   - Open the paper and lay it colored side up. If you have creased all folds well, the paper will be raised off the surface.
   - Take two adjacent corners and pull them together. Repeat with the opposite set of corners. You now have back-to-back triangles, or a star shape when opened slightly.

   Make 17 or more triangles.

2. Divide the paper triangles into three sets and string them on the pieces of string using the needle and thread. Put 3 beads or 6 Cheerios in between each triangle so that the triangles stay apart. Align the flaps of each triangle so that it fits into the slits of the triangle below it.

3. Tie the star strands to the stick.

4. Add a poem written on a long strip of paper to your stick.

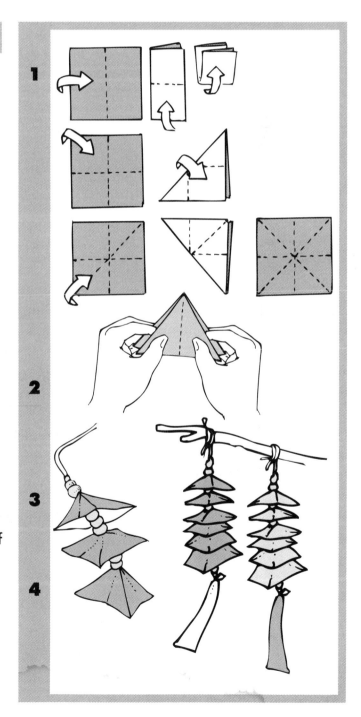

Make a Tin Lantern

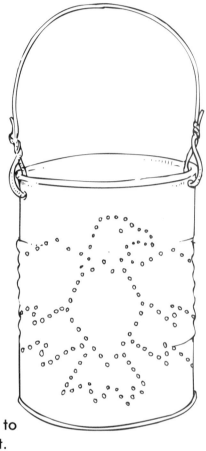

▶ Materials

- tin can (a one-pound coffee can size is best)
- patterns on page 32
- permanent marker
- water
- different sized nails
- hammer
- several layers of newspaper or a folded towel
- lightweight wire
- wire cutters
- candle

▶ Preparation

Remove all labels from the can. Remove the top; retain the bottom.

Before the holes can be punched, the can needs to be filled with water and the water frozen. This provides a more stable surface for hammering the nails.

You may need to make arrangements for this if you do not have access to a freezer at school. Elicit help from parents who live close to school. You may only be able to have a small group of students at a time do this project.

▶ Steps to Follow

1. Remove the can from the freezer. Tape the pattern to the can.

2. Place the can on several layers of newspaper or on a folded towel.

   Using a hammer and nail, hammer holes through the points on the pattern and into the can. Vary the size of holes by using different sized nails.

   Remove the pattern.

3. Make holes for a handle on opposite sides of the can rim.

   Set the can in a sink or tub so the ice can melt, or place the can under running water until the ice pulls away from the sides of the can. Discard the ice.

4. Cut wire a desired length for a handle. Wind through holes at can rim.

   Drip wax from a candle into the bottom of the lantern and mount the candle standing straight up.

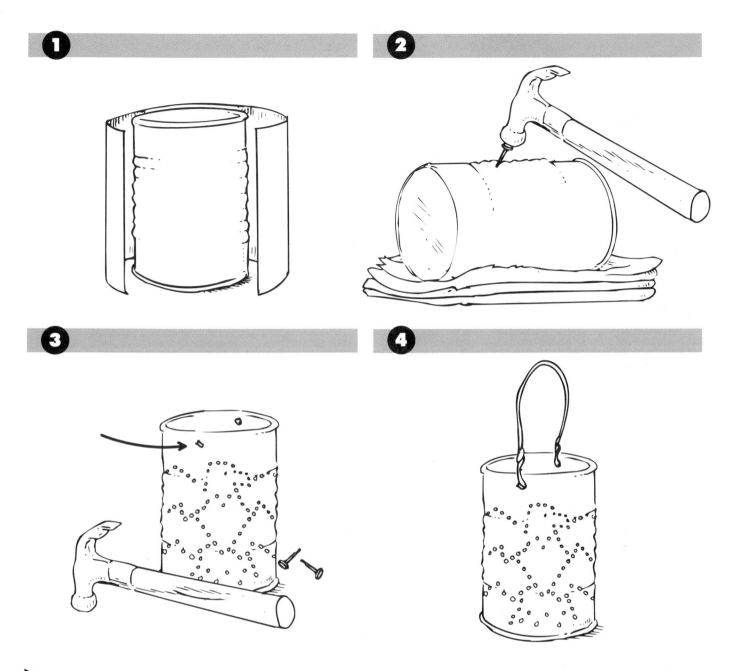

▶ Suggestions

- This activity requires the use of nails, hammers, and wire cutters. It should be conducted only with one or two students at a time and under direct adult supervision.
- Let students design their own pattern around a patriotic theme.
- Students may choose to randomly punch holes creating a swirling or abstract effect.
- Make dipped candles to use in your tin lanterns.